TANKS

John Willis

LET'S READ
AV²
BY WEIGL™
ADDED VALUE • AUDIO VISUAL

Go to www.av2books.com, and enter this book's unique code.

BOOK CODE

E239274

AV² by Weigl brings you media enhanced books that support active learning.

AV² provides enriched content that supplements and complements this book. Weigl's AV² books strive to create inspired learning and engage young minds in a total learning experience.

Your AV² Media Enhanced books come alive with...

Audio
Listen to sections of the book read aloud.

Video
Watch informative video clips.

Try This!
Complete activities and hands-on experiments.

Key Words
Study vocabulary, and complete a matching word activity.

Quizzes
Test your knowledge.

Slide Show
View images and captions, and prepare a presentation.

Embedded Weblinks
Gain additional information for research.

... and much, much more!

Published by AV² by Weigl
350 5th Avenue, 59th Floor New York, NY 10118
Website: www.av2books.com

Library of Congress Cataloging-in-Publication Data

Names: Willis, John, 1989- author.
Title: Tanks / John Willis.
Description: New York, NY : AV2 by Weigl, [2017] | Series: Mighty military machines | Includes index.
Identifiers: LCCN 2016034503 (print) | LCCN 2016034622 (ebook) | ISBN 9781489647696 (hard cover : alkaline paper) | ISBN 9781489650887 (soft cover : alkaline paper) | ISBN 9781489647702 (Multi-user ebk.)
Subjects: LCSH: Tanks (Military science)--Juvenile literature.
Classification: LCC UG446.5 .W487 2017 (print) | LCC UG446.5 (ebook) | DDC 623.74/752--dc23
LC record available at https://lccn.loc.gov/2016034503

Printed in the United States of America in Brainerd, Minnesota
1 2 3 4 5 6 7 8 9 0 20 19 18 17 16

082016
210716

Editor: Katie Gillespie
Art Director: Terry Paulhus

Weigl acknowledges Getty Images and Wikimedia Commons as the primary image suppliers for this title.

TANKS

CONTENTS

2 AV² Book Code
4 What Are Tanks?
6 Thick Armor
8 Top Turrets
10 Heavy Tracks
12 Tank Crews
14 First Tanks
16 Special Tools
18 Kinds of Tanks
20 Staying Safe
22 Tank Facts
24 Key Words

Tanks are heavy machines covered in armor. They are used by the United States military.

TF 1-64 AR

QTA 028 → C11
B 9049 ARM BN

6

The body of a tank is called its hull. It is made of thick armor to keep its crew safe.

Tanks have sloped armor. If an object hits this armor, it will bounce up and away from the tank.

Most tanks have a large turret on top of the hull. It can turn to face in any direction. This lets the tank aim in a different direction than it is moving.

The turret on an M1 Abrams tank is in the center of the hull.

9

Tank wheels run on tracks. When the wheels turn, they pull or push the tracks. The heavy tracks help tanks move across hills and ditches.

An M1 Abrams tank weighs more than nine elephants.

Many tanks have a crew of four soldiers. The commander decides what the tank and crew should do. The driver controls the tank from inside the hull.

The gunner aims the turret and the loader reloads the cannon.

13

Tanks were first made more than 100 years ago. The first two tanks were called "Little Willie" and "Big Willie."

The first tank designs were based on the way tractors move over rough ground.

EXIT

LITTLE WILLIE
~1915~

15

Some tanks have special tools. An M1 Abrams tank has smoke grenade launchers.

Six smoke grenades can make a smokescreen to keep the tank hidden.

The M104 Wolverine has a folding bridge on its top. The bridge is almost as long as two buses.

There are many different kinds of tanks. Assault Breacher Vehicles have a large plow or dozer blades on the front. They clear a safe path for other vehicles.

Riding in a tank can be dangerous. Tanks have special features to keep the crew safe.

TANK FACTS

These pages provide more detail about the interesting facts found in the book. They are intended to be used by adults as a learning support to help young readers round out their knowledge of each machine featured in the *Mighty Military Machines* series.

Pages 4–5

Tanks are heavy machines covered in armor. While there are many types of armored military vehicles, tanks are typically distinguished by their tracks, turret, and heavy armor. The U.S. Army first used tanks during World War I. Hundreds of French-produced FT-17 tanks were driven by U.S. forces. Today, the main battle tank of the U.S. Army and Marine Corps is the M1 Abrams.

Pages 6–7

The body of a tank is called its hull. Some tanks had metal plates as armor, up to 9.8 inches (250 millimeters) thick. Later designs included layers of different materials to make the tank more resistant to explosives. Modern reactive armor has a small layer of explosives between metal sheets. When struck, these plates explode outward, neutralizing some of the projectile's force.

Pages 8–9

Most tanks have a large turret on top of the hull.. The FT-17 was the first tank with a rotating turret. Modern tanks, such as the M1 Abrams, have their turret mounted in the center of the hull. A gear integrated into the hull allows the turret to rotate, providing a wide range of fire without requiring the tank to move or change direction.

Pages 10–11

Tank wheels run on tracks. Tank tracks are looped around the wheel-like sprockets on each side of the vehicle. As they turn, the track moves along the ground. Tank tracks have a much larger surface area touching the ground than the wheels of a car, so they can grip surfaces more effectively. To turn, a tank moves one track more slowly than the other.

Pages 12–13

Many tanks have a crew of four soldiers. The driver uses periscopes to see outside the tank. The gunner and commander also use a range of periscopes, as well as night vision and other sensors to perceive the battlefield. Loaders are responsible for supplying the cannon with different types of ammunition, often as requested by the gunner.

Pages 14–15

Tanks were first made more than 100 years ago. Little Willie was too slow and unmaneuverable on the battlefield. Big Willie was officially known as "His Majesty's Landship, Tank Mk 1." The term "tank" tricked enemies into thinking the vehicle was a mobile water tank. The Mk 1's rhomboid-shaped tracks allowed it to pass over trenches more than 9 feet (2.7 meters) wide.

Pages 16–17

Some tanks have special tools. The M250 grenade launcher system consists of two launchers near the turret. Depending on weather conditions, between 6 and 12 smoke grenades are needed to hide an M1 Abrams.

Pages 18–19

There are many different kinds of tanks. Assault Breacher Vehicles (ABVs) clear paths through minefields. ABVs have two rocket launchers to detonate mines at a distance. Their frontal plows clear obstacles quickly. The M104 Wolverine is an unarmed, two-person vehicle that can set up a portable bridge in five minutes. From the other side, it can retrieve the bridge for later use.

Pages 20–21

Riding in a tank can be dangerous. Tanks provide an armored, mobile platform for a large amount of firepower. The M1 Abrams is a durable tank. In addition to external armor, the sealed crew area has air filters to protect against chemical weapons. The ammunition is stored in armored compartments, and there is an automatic fire extinguishing system to keep the crew safe.

KEY WORDS

Research has shown that as much as 65 percent of all written material published in English is made up of 300 words. These 300 words cannot be taught using pictures or learned by sounding them out. They must be recognized by sight. This book contains 60 common sight words to help young readers improve their reading fluency and comprehension. This book also teaches young readers several important content words, such as proper nouns. These words are paired with pictures to aid in learning and improve understanding.

Page	Sight Words First Appearance
4	are, by, in, the, they, used
7	a, an, and, away, from, have, if, is, it, its, keep, made, of, this, to, up, will
8	any, can, different, face, large, lets, most, on, than
11	help, more, move, or, run, when
12	do, four, many, should, what
14	first, over, two, way, were, years
16	has, some
17	make
18	almost, as, long
19	for, kinds, other, there
20	be

Page	Content Words First Appearance
4	armor, machines, military, tanks
7	body, crew, hull, object
8	center, direction, M1 Abrams, top, turret
11	ditches, elephants, hills, tracks, wheels
12	cannon, commander, driver, gunner, loader, soldiers
14	Big Willie, designs, ground, Little Willie, tractors
16	smoke grenade launchers, tools
17	smoke grenades, smokescreen
18	bridge, buses, M104 Wolverine
19	Assault Breacher Vehicles, dozer blades, front, path, plow

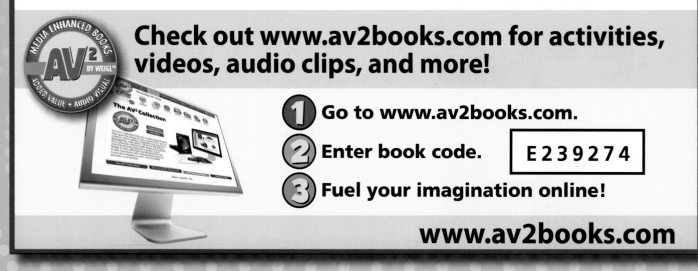